D1306134

ART PROFILES
For Kids

MANET

Mitchell Lane

PUBLISHERS

P.O. Box 196

Hockessin, Delaware 19707

Visit us on the web: www.mitchelllane.com

Comments? email us: mitchelllane@mitchelllane.com

ART PROFILES FOR KIDS

Titles in the Series

Canaletto
Claude Monet
Edvard Munch
Leonardo da Vinci
Manet
Michelangelo
Paul Cézanne
Pablo Picasso
Pierre-Auguste Renoir
Raphael
Rembrandt
Vincent van Gogh

Art Profiles
For Kids

MANET

Kathleen Tracy

Mitchell Lane
PUBLISHERS

P.O. Box 196
Hockessin, Delaware 19707
Visit us on the web: www.mitchelllane.com
Comments? email us: mitchelllane@mitchelllane.com

Mitchell Lane
PUBLISHERS

Printing 1   2   3   4   5   6   7   8   9

Library of Congress Cataloging-in-Publication Data
Tracy, Kathleen.
  Edouard Manet / by Kathleen Tracy.
      p. cm.—(Art profiles for kids)
  Includes bibliographical references and index.
  ISBN 978-1-58415-746-5 (library bound)
  1. Manet, Édouard, 1832–1883—Juvenile literature. 2. Painters—France—Biography—Juvenile literature. I. Manet, Édouard, 1832–1883. II. Title.
  ND553.M3T68 2009
  759.4—dc22
  [B]
                                                                    2009001321

ABOUT THE AUTHOR: Kathleen Tracy has been a journalist for over twenty years. Her writing has been featured in magazines including *The Toronto Star*'s "Star Week," *A&E Biography* magazine, *KidScreen* and *TV Times*. She is also the author of numerous books for Mitchell Lane Publishers, including *William Hewlett: Pioneer of the Computer Age; The Fall of the Berlin Wall; Paul Cézanne; The Story of September 11, 2001; Johnny Depp; Mariah Carey;* and *Kelly Clarkson*.

ABOUT THE COVER: The images on the cover are paintings by the various artists in this series.

PUBLISHER'S NOTE: The facts on which this story is based have been thoroughly researched. Documentation of such research appears on page 46. While every possible effort has been made to ensure accuracy, the publisher will not assume liability for damages caused by inaccuracies in the data, and makes no warranty on the accuracy of the information contained herein.

PLB

Art Profiles for Kids

Chapter One
Très Scandal 7
For Your Information: *Le Déjeuner sur l'Herbe* 11

Chapter Two
Unlikely Provocateur 13
For Your Information: Diego Velázquez 19

Chapter Three
Early Works 21
For Your Information: Charles Baudelaire 27

Chapter Four
Inspirations 29
For Your Information: Edgar Degas 35

Chapter Five
An Untimely End 37
For Your Information: Monet 42

Chapter Notes 43
Chronology 44
Selected Paintings 44
Timeline in History 45
Further Reading 46
    Books 46
    Works Consulted 46
    On the Internet 46
Glossary 47
Index 48

Le Déjeuner sur l'Herbe (The Picnic) was based on two Renaissance paintings: Raphael's *The Judgment of Paris* and Titian's *Concert Champetre*. Nudes were a common subject in classical painting, but Manet's depiction of a nude woman in a modern setting was considered so scandalous, the judges at Paris' most prestigious art exhibition rejected it for their yearly show.

one

Trés Scandal

It was a scandal that rocked the Parisian art community. It also introduced a new painting style that would revolutionize nineteenth-century art.

In the 1860s, the most important event of the French art world was the annual Salon, a public art show that could make or break a young painter's career. Because so many influential people attended the Salon, the competition to get a painting exhibited was fierce—and frustrating. Most members of the selection committee were conservative academics who did not encourage originality. They wanted paintings that were true to the style and artistic philosophies of the classical Renaissance paint-ers, so artists such as Édouard Manet were viewed as upstarts with questionable talent. In 1863, Manet's controversial *Déjeuner sur l'Herbe* (*The Picnic,* or its literal translation, *Lunch on the Grass*) had been resoundingly rejected by the jury, which labeled the painting obscene. Nearly three thousand other works—an extremely high number—were also rejected.

The jury's rejection of so many artists created a heated public contro-versy that escalated to the point where Emperor Napoleon III felt he had to get involved. He was worried the artistic showdown might become a political cause célèbre. To defuse the outcry, he established the Salon des Refusés, an exhibit featuring works refused by the main Salon. Natu-rally, many people attended the Salon des Refusés just to see firsthand the source of all the controversy. Regardless of any negative press, the publicity helped validate the emerging Impressionist movement. The

centerpiece of that first Salon des Refusés was Manet's *Déjeuner sur l'Herbe,* which depicted clothed men picnicking outdoors with a nude woman. Today, the painting seems almost quaint, a snapshot of a bygone era. But at the time, the idea of placing a naked woman in a contemporary setting was considered outrageously improper.

Considering the scandal *Le Déjeuner sur l'Herbe* caused, Manet waited two years before submitting another painting for Salon consideration. To his surprise, the jury agreed to show *Olympia* in the 1865 Salon. Art historians now suspect the Salon jury selected *Olympia* for political reasons: Although they did not believe it up to their classical standards, they did not want to be accused again of censorship or narrow-minded thinking. They decided to let the public judge for themselves. Curiously, though, Manet did not view himself as an outsider. He was influenced and inspired by traditional artists and themes; he just wanted to put his own contemporary spin on those themes.

When the exhibit opened, the uproar was deafening. Manet was vilified for the painting's revolutionary style and subject presentation. *Olympia* shows a woman reclining on a bed, nude except for a slipper on her left foot—the slipper on her right foot has fallen off—a bow around her neck, a bracelet, and a pink flower in her hair. There is a black cat at the foot of the bed, and a maid is presenting flowers to her. Although nudes were common subjects in art, it was the realism of the painting, and the fact that Olympia is probably a prostitute—the flowers are presumably from a waiting client—that upset the public's nineteenth-century sensibilities.

Adding to the realism of the painting was the way Manet used strong brushstrokes and "impressions" of shapes and forms rather than detailing each aspect of the painting. "*Olympia* shocked in every possible way," notes art historian Linda Nochlin in the film *Shock of the Nude.* "That is to say formally, morally, in terms of its subject matter. It had the whole range of outrage."[1]

Art historian Kenneth Clark added that the picture did more than outrage viewers; it made them uncomfortable because it hit so close to

When *Olympia* was exhibited in 1865, it was condemned by critics as obscene. Today it is considered a masterpiece of early Impressionist style.

home. "For almost the first time since the Renaissance, a painting of the nude represented a real woman in probable surroundings. . . . Amateurs were thus suddenly reminded of the circumstances under which actual nudity was familiar to them and their embarrassment is understandable."[2]

Writer Antonin Proust, Manet's longtime friend, later observed, "If the canvas of the *Olympia* was not destroyed, it is only because of the precautions that were taken by the administration."[3]

Manet's depiction of nude women in relatable settings in *Olympia* and *Le Déjeuner sur l'Herbe* was so revolutionary, he is considered the first modernist painter. But while it was Manet's talent that brought *Olympia* to life, it was the model he chose, Victorine Meurent, who gave the painting its visceral punch. Victorine came from a creative family—her mother made hats and women's accessories, and her father was a bronze-worker. She began working as a model when she was just sixteen, posing over the years for many famous artists, including Alfred Stevens, Edgar Degas, and Henri de Toulouse-Lautrec. She also sang at the cafés and gave guitar and violin lessons.

She met Manet after he saw her walking down the street carrying a guitar and was struck by her red hair and small stature. He re-created that first impression in their first collaboration, *The Street Singer,* in 1862 when she was eighteen. She was also his model in *Le Déjeuner sur l'Herbe.*

In the early 1870s, Victorine began taking art classes, and a short time later she and Manet became estranged—after she posed for his 1873 painting *Gare Saint-Lazare (The Railway).* In an ironic twist, three years after she stopped modeling for Manet, Victorine submitted her work to the Salon and was accepted. That same year, the jury rejected Manet's submissions.

While Victorine suffered no apparent consequence from posing in two highly controversial paintings, Manet was crushed by the criticism of his work. In a letter to a friend, French poet Charles Pierre Baudelaire, he wrote, "They are raining insults on me. Someone must be wrong."[4]

Time would prove Manet right. Over the next two decades, he would help define Impressionism, in both style and content.

"Manet has given us an incredible gift," said New York artist Mike Bidlo, "this idea that art is something which kind of rattles your cage or takes you to another area of intellectual understanding. He was exploring the role of artist as provocateur."[5]

Manet's refusal to conform to the status quo would become an inspiration for generations of artists to follow.

Le Déjeuner sur l'Herbe

While *Olympia* may be the most famous of Manet's paintings, *Le Déjeuner sur l'Herbe* might be the most influential overall. The painting was not done in an Impressionistic style, but its break from conformity laid the foundation for the Impressionist movement's evolution.

A large canvas measuring 7 feet x 8_ feet, the painting was exhibited at the Salon de Refusés under the name *Le Bain (The Bath)*. (Manet renamed it *Le Déjeuner sur l'Herbe* in 1867.) Manet got the idea for the painting one day while he and his friend Antonin Proust were watching swimmers near the Seine in Argenteuil, a Paris suburb. He was also inspired by Giorgione's classical painting *Fête Champêtre (The Picnic)*, which set the precedent of depicting nude women alongside clothed men, and which Manet had copied as an art exercise while studying under French artist Thomas Couture.

According to Proust, Manet announced: "I want to re-do it [*Fête Champêtre*] and to re-do it with a transparent atmosphere with people like those you see over there. I know it's going to be attacked but they can say what they like."[6]

His models for the painting were Victorine Meurent as the nude woman, again looking directly at the viewer with an enigmatic expression on her face, unabashed with her nudity; his brother-in-law, who is seated next to Victorine; and his brother Eugène, who is pointing at the couple. Like *Olympia*, the controversy over *Le Déjeuner sur l'Herbe* stemmed from the context in which Manet's nude women appeared. Up to that time, nude women were depicted in either historical or mythological settings. The size of the canvas added to the feeling of the observer literally walking into the picnic.

Portrait of Victorine Meurent by Manet, 1862

Manet's innovative use of lighting was a precursor to the *en plein air* style that would be a hallmark of Impressionism. It inspired works by Paul Cézanne, Pablo Picasso and Claude Monet. Monet in fact worked on his own versions of *Le Déjeuner sur l'Herbe*—minus the nudity.

Manet's father was a stern man; his mother an unhappy, discontented housewife. His stark 1860 portrait of his parents—called *M. and Mme. Auguste Manet*—powerfully captures the dynamic of their marriage.

two

Unlikely Provocateur

Édouard Manet would never be a starving artist. Perhaps because he did not have to worry about earning a living from his art, he felt free to follow his creative instincts rather than conform to what critics and the general public thought art should be. But little about Manet's family and childhood indicated he would grow up to be one of the most influential artists in history.

The Manets were French blue-bloods, the equivalent of New York high society. His father, Auguste, worked at the Ministry of Justice as a civil court judge. Acquaintances described him as honest but self-righteous. His mother, Eugénie Désirée, was born in Sweden. Her godfather was French-born Jean-Baptiste Bernadotte, who was later crowned King of Sweden and served as Charles XIV. Just twenty years old when she married, Eugénie was fourteen years younger than Auguste. If Manet's later portraits of his parents are any indication, it was not a particularly joyous marriage.

Édouard was born in Paris on January 23, 1832. He had two brothers: Eugéne, born a year later, and Gustave, born in 1835. Through Auguste's income as a jurist and Eugénie's considerable dowry, the Manets were quite wealthy. They lived in a four-story Left Bank apartment house across the street from L'École des Beaux-Arts, the top art school in France at the time. However, Auguste was not a patron of the arts, and he expected all his sons to pursue white-collar professional careers, envisioning Édouard as an attorney.

When he was seven, Manet attended a parochial school run by a priest named Abbé Poiloup. When he was twelve, he was sent to Collège Rollin, the equivalent of high school. The principal, Mr. Defauconpret, was a friend of Auguste and had socialized many times at their house. Even though the school was within walking distance of his home, Édouard boarded at Rollin, but spent Thursdays and Sundays at home. The curriculum was strenuous, with classes in physics, chemistry, biology, math, history, debate, philosophy, literature, Greek, Latin, and either German or English. While there he met Antonin Proust, who became his lifelong friend. Proust later described the depressing environment of the place, which was once a girls' reform school: "There was an ill-lit, prison-like room, stinking of smoky lamps in the evening furnished in the most primitive manner with narrow, rough benches, screwed so close to desks that they crushed your chest. We were packed in there like sardines."[1]

Édouard was a mostly indifferent student; the only academic class he enjoyed was history—on one of Manet's report cards, Defauconpret referred to him as feeble but enthusiastic. Physically, though, he was athletic enough to participate in gymnastics. He was also interested in drawing, which his maternal uncle Edmond Fournier strongly supported and encouraged. In fact, it was Edmond who paid for the extracurricular drawing class offered by Rollin; Auguste thought it was a waste of money, since he intended

Antonin Proust, painted by Manet

for Édouard to be a lawyer. Ironically, Manet felt constrained by the class, which primarily had him sketching classical statues. He much preferred drawing the boys in his class and other things in his immediate surround-

ings. When he got caught he was suspended from the class for a month, but it was clear Manet was already an independent thinker when it came to his art.

Manet's lack of interest in his studies caused tension with his father, and although Édouard always shared a warm relationship with his mother, he tended to be as unhappy when he was at home as he was when he was at school. Some of the few bright spots were outings with Uncle Edmond, who lived in the same building as Manet and his family. Edmond was the antithesis of Auguste—cheerful, openly affectionate, and outgoing. He was also passionate about art. Edmond regularly took Édouard, and sometimes Antonin, to muse-

The Louvre is one of the premier art museums in the world. The original structure was a fort, built in the 1190s, but it has housed the museum since 1793.

ums. At the Louvre, Manet became enamored by the work of Spanish painter Diego Velásquez, who would have a significant influence on Manet's later painting style.

The disagreement over Édouard's future came to a head in 1847, when he was fifteen. Auguste wanted Édouard to enroll in law school, but the teen refused, informing his father he wanted to be an artist. Then it was Auguste's turn to refuse. Finally they reached a compromise: Édouard would apply to naval college to pursue a career at sea. He loved the ocean and it would get him out of Rollin and out of his house.

In July 1847 he took the entrance examination . . . and failed. However, if he spent time aboard a commercial ship that traveled to the other side of the equator, and if he was still under eighteen when he applied, the college would accept him. Édouard and a group of other teenagers paid to travel on the merchant vessel *Havre et Guadeloupe* on a voyage to Rio de Janeiro, Brazil. While on board, the teens would also be tutored by instructors hired to prepare them for a retest of the admission exam.

Édouard and the other students set sail on December 8, 1848. The night before, he wrote a letter to his mother that was full of excitement and optimism over the coming adventure. He called the *Havre et Guadeloupe* a "magnificent vessel where we will be as comfortable as can be; we shall not only have the essentials but even more, a degree of luxury and all the comforts to console and reassure the sad mamas who came to see their children off."[2]

He wrote home every couple of days, the letters becoming a kind of journal. It didn't take long for the newness to wear off. Every day was the same: rising at six-thirty, spending five hours in class, dinner at four, recreation until seven, study hall until bedtime at nine. After just a couple of weeks, Édouard found time slowly dragging by.

"How boring is the life of a sailor," he wrote. "Nothing but sky and water, always the same thing, it's stupid; we can't do a thing, our teachers are sick and

Rio de Janeiro, the capital of Brazil, is on the Atlantic Coast. Because it is below the equator, it was summer there during Manet's visit. Manet described the weather as stifling hot.

On his voyage to Brazil in 1848, Manet drew Porto Santo Island and sent the picture to his mother.

the rolling is so bad that you can't stay below deck. Sometimes at dinner we fall on top of each other and the platters full of food with us."[3] Adding to his homesickness was the length of the trip. It was supposed to take four months round-trip, but bad weather was causing delays—and as a result, food was being rationed. The only upside was that Manet liked the uniforms they were given to wear.

The ship finally reached Rio on February 5, 1849. Once anchored in calm waters, the teens no longer had to spend their days fighting seasickness and constant motion, but they were still bored. Édouard was unable to find a French-speaking instructor in the city, so to help pass the time, the captain suggested Édouard give drawing lessons to the others on board.

"Here I am elevated to the rank of drawing master; I must tell you that during the crossing I made a name for myself; all the officers and teachers had me do caricatures of them and the captain himself asked me for one to give his family as a Christmas present. I had the good fortune in all of this to perform to everybody's satisfaction."[4] Whether Édouard was simply recounting pride in his achievement or making a point to his father is

A photograph of Rio de Janeiro, taken around 1865. The city had been founded 300 years earlier by Estácio de Sá, a Portuguese soldier and officer, who established the town as a military base.

unclear. What is clear is that his confidence as an artist was given a significant boost by being named the ship's art teacher.

On the two days a week students were allowed to go ashore and explore Rio—which at the time was the largest city in South America—Manet walked the streets soaking up the local atmosphere. His most lasting impression, though, was the social order; specifically, the treatment of blacks. "All . . . are slaves; all these poor creatures look downtrodden; the power that whites have over them is extraordinary. I saw a slave market; for us this is really a revolting sight. . . . The Negroes have only a pair of trousers for clothing, sometimes a linen jacket, but as slaves they are not allowed to wear shoes. The Negresses are naked to the waist, some wear a scarf that falls over the chest."[5] Only whites were referred to as Brazilian.

The trip to Brazil and back took six months. When Édouard returned to France in June 1849, he was no longer a boy; during his time away he had matured into a young man who knew what he wanted. And with the help of Uncle Edmond, Édouard finally received his father's blessing to pursue a career in art.

Diego Velázquez

During Diego Velázquez's lifetime, his fame was confined to Spain. It wasn't until after his death that appreciation for his body of work spread throughout Europe. By the time Manet first became acquainted in the nineteenth century with Velázquez's work, Velázquez was considered one of the great artists in history. Unfortunately, very little has been written about his personal life, especially his childhood.

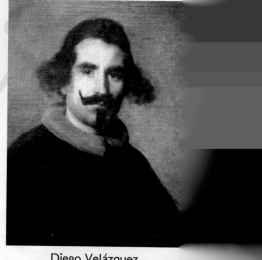

Diego Velázquez,
Self-Portrait, 1630

Diego Rodriguez de Silva y Velázquez was born in Seville, Spain, but the exact date is not known. His birth date is often listed as June 6, 1599, the day he was baptized at the church of San Pedro. He was the eldest of seven children born to Juan Rodriguez de Silva, a lawyer descended from Portuguese nobility, and Geronima Velázquez.

Velázquez showed a talent for art at a young age. After a brief apprenticeship with Spanish painter Francisco de Herrera the Elder, who worked in both the Mannerist and Baroque styles, Velázquez began studying under Francisco Pacheco in 1611. (It's not known for a fact that he apprenticed with Herrera, although many biographers believe he did.) Pacheco was an unimaginative painter, strictly adhering to traditional concepts, but he was well connected with the royal court and others who could help establish Diego's career.

Velázquez was accepted into the painters' guild of St. Luke in Seville in 1617. A year later he married Pacheco's daughter Juana, and they moved to Madrid. When he was twenty-five, Velázquez painted a portrait of Philip IV, who subsequently became the young artist's patron. Except for two trips to Italy in 1629 and 1649, Velázquez spent the rest of his life working primarily for the royal court, which is why his work was relatively unknown through the rest of Europe until the nineteenth century.

His paintings, particularly his portraits, are known for their realism, the quality that inspired Manet. He once said, "I would rather be the first painter of common things than second in higher art."[6]

In 1660, Velásquez contracted a fever, possibly typhoid, and died on August 6. His wife, Juana, died eight days later. They were interred together in a family vault at the Church of San Juan Bautista. The church was destroyed in 1811, and today there is no record of where Velásquez is buried.

Self-Portrait with Palette, 1879. Although Manet was very serious about his painting, he had an outgoing personality and enjoyed socializing in cafés with other artists. He was considered one of the most intelligent of the Parisian artists.

three

Early Works

In 1850, Édouard began studying with Thomas Couture, a popular art teacher at the time. The artistic version of a one-hit wonder, Couture was best known for *The Romans of the Decadence*, a large canvas depicting a party of debauchery. The painting was the talk of the 1847 Salon, and he was soon in demand as an instructor. Chubby and short with unruly thick hair and a gruff demeanor, Couture was skilled technically but lacked the creative genius that separates good painters from great artists. The potential the Salon jury saw in Couture never materialized.

Couture's class was limited to a maximum of 30 students, each of whom paid a yearly tuition of 120 francs—almost $12,000 in today's money—for the privilege. The artist visited the students twice a week to offer critique and criticism. According to Proust, Couture was a disengaged teacher. "Couture came to visit us twice a week; he glanced at our studies with a distracted eye, ordered a break, rolled himself a cigarette, told some stories about his master [Antoine Jean] Gros, then took himself off."[1]

Manet was frustrated by Couture's traditional academic approach to painting. He frequently clashed with the models hired because their poses were stiff and

Couture's *The Romans of the Decadence*, 1847

mannered instead of natural. At one point, Manet was so irritated, he quit—but he returned a month later at the insistence of his father. Although his mood had not improved, Édouard realized Couture's studio offered him the chance to learn basic drawing and painting techniques. Once he learned the craft of painting, he could use that knowledge to create his art.

Over the next six years, Manet took short trips around Europe, in part to experience the local cultures and keep abreast of contemporary art movements and trends. He also spent time copying paintings done by old masters. He finally left Couture's tutelage in 1856 to set up his own studio on the Rue Lavoisier. He spent much of 1857 at the Louvre copying paintings by Titian and Velázquez. A year later he created *The Boy with Cherries* (c. 1858), which became his first painting of note but has an infamous back story. The model was a young boy named Alexander whom Manet had hired to be his studio assistant. One day after Manet had accused the boy of stealing, Alexander hanged himself in the studio, and Manet found the body. He was so upset he moved to a new studio. The incident inspired one of Baudelaire's "prose poems," *La Corde (The Rope).*[2]

In 1859 Manet submitted *The Absinthe Drinker* to the Salon, much to the dismay of his former teacher. Although Couture believed that artists should paint contemporary life and that art should relate to an artist's own experience, when confronted

Manet's model for *The Boy with Cherries*, painted in 1858, was his young assistant Alexander.

by *The Absinthe Drinker*—a stark depiction of an alcoholic—Couture was offended. He complained: "How can you paint anything so abominable? My poor friend, you are the absinthe drinker, you are the one who has lost his moral sense."[3]

The Salon jury agreed with Couture and rejected *The Absinthe Drinker*. Manet's father, however, was angered by the teacher's criticism and showed his son unexpected support. Auguste wasn't the only one whom Couture alienated. He later had a falling out with Napoleon, who had wanted Couture to work for him. And he offended many members of the art scene with his criticisms of Eugéne Delacroix, who is considered the father of the French romantic art movement. Although some of his other paintings were nicely received, Couture never achieved greatness or even respect. Over time, even his *Romans of the Decadence* became considered a lesser work. Bitter, he eventually gave up painting and became a recluse at his home outside of Paris. He died in 1879.

Manet believed art should depict real life, not idealized life. The bleak imagery of his 1858 painting *The Absinthe Drinker* was deemed too realistic and was rejected by the Salon.

Manet, on the other hand, did not let criticism stop him from doggedly following his vision. Nor did he hide himself away. Because he lived off family money, Manet had the freedom to eat and drink wherever he wanted, and he enjoyed the company of the leading artists and writers of the time. Among his friends were poet and art critic Charles Baudelaire, art critic and collector Théodore Duret, and writer Émile Zola, who would be a staunch supporter of the Impressionists.

Manet's 1861 entries to the Salon were *M. and Mme. Auguste Manet*, an unflinching portrait of his parents, and *The Spanish Singer*. Both were accepted, and *The Spanish Singer* won an honorable mention. But the early 1860s would be a time of professional and

The Spanish Singer by Manet was given honorable mention at the 1861 Salon.

personal transition for Manet. As his artistic vision and style matured—as seen in *Le Déjeuner sur l'Herbe* and *Olympia*—he would encounter criticism and outrage from the art mainstream status quo.

Manet's father spent the last years of his life in ill health due to complications from syphilis. In December 1857, Auguste suffered partial paralysis, and although he recuperated enough to walk again, the disease spread to his brain, leaving him unable to talk. Auguste died in 1862.

A year later, Manet surprised Baudelaire by announcing he was getting married to Suzanne Leenhoff—nobody had been aware Manet had a mistress. But there may have been a reason for his discretion.

Leenhoff was born in the Netherlands in 1829 and came to Paris when she was nineteen. Described as attractive, even-tempered, and plump, she was hired in late 1849 to teach the Manet boys piano and subsequently started an affair with Auguste. In January 1852, she gave birth to a son she named Léon. Most historians believe the child's father was Auguste. To hide his illegitimacy, Léon was passed off as Suzanne's younger brother, and when Léon was baptized in 1855, Édouard and Suzanne were listed as his godparents.

At some point Suzanne ended her relationship with Auguste and became Édouard's mistress. By 1860, she and Léon were living with Édouard in his Paris apartment. Suzanne and Édouard were married in October 1863. Théodore Duret liked Suzanne, calling her "a woman of artistic taste, able to understand [Manet] and to give him that support and encouragement which helped him better withstand the attacks made upon him."[4]

Even so, the *Olympia* debacle in 1865 left Manet upset and restless. In a letter to Baudelaire, he admitted, "I wish I had you here . . . insults are beating down on me like hail. I've never been through anything like it."[5]

He was not an agitator by nature and had not meant to stir up controversy. Many people were surprised when they met Manet to discover he was well dressed, well mannered, and amiable—not the radical bohemian his work suggested. To recharge, he took a trip to Spain in August 1865 and, as he'd hoped, got creative inspiration and validation from Diego Velázquez.

Las Meninas (The Maids of Honor), c. 1656, by Velázquez

Manet painted *Portrait of Émile Zola* in 1868. Zola was a French journalist and author who supported the Impressionist movement.

"What thrilled me most in Spain and made the whole trip worthwhile were the works of Velázquez," Manet wrote in another letter. "He's the greatest artist of all . . . and the sight of those masterpieces gave me enormous hope and courage."[6]

Although he was supposed to stay in Spain a month, he cut his visit short primarily because he found Spanish food inedible. The bad cuisine led to a new friendship—he met Théodore Duret after arguing about food at the Grand Hotel de Paris in Madrid, and they eventually became close friends.

While his brief vacation may have improved his outlook, his reputation as an artistic rebel continued in 1866 when the Salon rejected two more of his works. Duret once explained why Manet's style was so jarring to the Salon jury: "His contemporaries avoided brilliancy of color, blended different tones together or shrouded the outlines in shadow. Manet, on the other hand, suppressed the shadows, painted everything in luminous tone, put the boldest, the most incisive colors in immediate juxtaposition."[7]

Émile Zola also came to Manet's defense. He wrote several articles praising the artist and predicted: "Manet's place is destined to be in the Louvre."[8]

For the time being, Manet would have been satisfied to simply find acceptance of his work. Eventually, the ongoing criticism would push the normally mild-mannered artist to the brink.

Charles Baudelaire

Charles Baudelaire is considered one of the most influential poets of the nineteenth century. His introspective, frequently dark verses reflected a life filled with drama and, in the end, despair.

Born in Paris on April 9, 1821, Baudelaire was an only child. His father, François, was an ex-priest who was sixty when he married twenty-six-year-old Caroline Dufayis. François dabbled in writing poetry and painting and passed his love of the arts on to his son. After François died in 1827, Caroline married career soldier Major Jacques Aupick.

While Aupick was posted in Lyons, Charles attended the Collège Royal. When they returned to Paris in 1836, he enrolled at the Lycèe Louis-le-Grand and began writing poetry. Like Manet, his work was not well received—his instructors felt the emotions expressed in his poems were depraved. Baudelaire became moody and rebellious. He was expelled from the school in April 1839 and started spending most of his time in the Latin Quarter, making literary contacts and enjoying the bohemian lifestyle. It was probably during this time that Baudelaire contracted syphilis, the disease that would eventually kill him.

Aupick did not approve of his stepson's lifestyle, so in June 1841 he sent Charles on a voyage to India. Baudelaire didn't make it. He disembarked at Mauritius, an island off the east coast of Africa, and returned to Paris in February 1842. Later that year he started a romance with actress Jeanne Duval. Their lifelong, tumultuous relationship inspired some of Baudelaire's most passionate poetry.

His first collection of poems, *Les Fleurs du Mal*, was published in 1857. Thirteen of the 100 poems were deemed obscene, and Baudelaire was put on trial. Six of the poems were ordered removed from the book, and the poet was fined 300 francs. The book was a commercial flop and left Baudelaire with a feeling of failure. After his publisher went bankrupt, Baudelaire moved to Brussels, where he lived in poverty. He fell ill in 1866, suffering from aphasia and paralysis caused by advancing syphilis. He spent the last year of his life in a nursing home and died August 31, 1867. He was forty-six years old.

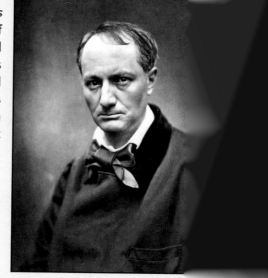

Charles Baudelaire

The Philosopher (*Beggar with Oysters*) is an homage to Velázquez, who frequently used full-length portraiture in his work. While not truly Impressionistic, the painting's loose brushstrokes would inspire the young artists who started the Impressionist movement.

four

Inspirations

When his submissions to the 1867 World's Fair in Paris were rejected, Manet decided to promote his art on his own. He borrowed 12,000 francs from his mother, the equivalent of more than $50,000 in today's money, and built a pavilion just outside the fairgrounds. There he held a private exhibition of 50 paintings.

Manet once told Proust that for paintings to be truly understood, they all needed to be viewed together, and he believed this was a chance for that to happen. Unfortunately, Manet only succeeded in opening his work to more ridicule. Proust later recalled, "Husbands drove their wives to the Pont de l'Alma. Feeling it was too fine an opportunity to pass up, they came to treat themselves and their families to a good laugh. Every self-respecting painter in Paris turned up at the Manet Exhibition. They all went wild with laughter. . . . All the papers without exception followed their lead."[1]

Even if Manet could not curry the favor of critics, he was well regarded among the young artists he befriended at the Café Guerbois, located in Paris' Montmartre neighborhood. The café offered locals a place to eat, drink, play billiards, and talk. Noisy and smoky, it became a favorite meeting spot for a group of upstart artists who admired Manet—Edgar Degas, Claude Monet, Auguste Renoir, Frédéric Bazille, Camille Pissarro, and Paul Cézanne—and who eventually formed the core of the Impressionist movement. Joining them were writers and art lovers, including Émile Zola, Théodore Duret, and novelist and art critic Louis Duranty. At the center

of the group was Manet, who, beginning around 1868, regularly held court with the younger artists and often engaged them in spirited conversations. The eldest, wealthiest, and best educated, Manet had few intellectual equals among the group, the exceptions being Pissarro, Bazille, and Degas. Sometimes the discussions turned angry; once, the situation almost turned deadly.

In February 1870, Manet reached the breaking point. In his review about an art exhibition that opened on February 18, Duranty included only one sentence about the two Manet paintings on display: "Manet showed a philosopher trampling oyster shells and a watercolor of his *Christ with Angels.*"[2] At face value, the comment seemed marginally snarky at worst, but Manet exploded. He strode into Café Guerbois and slapped Duranty, then challenged him to a duel using swords. Duranty accepted.

Portrait of Edmond [Louis] Duranty by Degas, 1879. Upset at critic Duranty's dismissive review of his work, Manet challenged him to a duel.

The duel was held at 11:00 A.M. on February 23 in Saint-Germain forest. Zola was Manet's second. According to the police report, "A single engagement took place and it was of such violence that both swords were badly bent. Monsieur Duranty received a slight wound below his right breast, his opponent's sword having glanced his side."[3] Seeing the wound, the seconds declared that honor had been satisfied and that there was no need to prolong the duel.

Amazingly, Manet and Duranty quickly reconciled, and the duel became part of Montmartre lore. The Café Guerbois regulars even composed a song in honor of their swordfight. Coincidental or not, a short time later Duranty wrote a glowing article about Manet, further cementing their repaired friendship.

Although nobody was severely hurt in the duel and the two men settled their differences, the incident exposed a darker side to Manet's personality that was rarely seen in public. Other traits, however, were very much on display, such as his independent approach to painting. In addition to employing professional models, Manet used people from all walks of life to pose in his work, including family and street people, most notably a local drunk named Collardet, who posed for *The Absinthe Drinker*. Manet even painted other artists, including Berthe Morisot—the woman many believe was the true love of Manet's life.

Fellow artist Henri Fantin-Latour introduced Manet to Morisot and her sister Edma in 1868. Édouard was thirty-six; Berthe was twenty-seven and an aspiring artist. Like most men at the time, Manet held the chauvinistic view that women only dabbled in art as a diversion instead of being driven by personal creative passion. But even at her young age, Berthe had already exhibited her paintings—she was the first woman to join the Impressionist movement and would exhibit at all but one of the group's exhibitions. Despite her interest in Impressionism, she was also influenced by Manet's style. In turn, he was influenced by her. She encouraged him to work outdoors in natural light, a style she had learned when studying under a well-regarded French landscapist named Camille Corot. Berthe also challenged Manet if she did not like his direction when she was posing for him.

Manet's confidante and mistress Berthe Morisot posed for eleven of his paintings, including *The Balcony* in 1868. She is seated with a fan.

The Manet and Morisot families became friends, and Berthe's letters to her sister strongly suggest her friendship with Édouard deepened into love and they became discreet lovers. Their emotional devotion to one another was no secret. She appeared in his painting *The Balcony* (she is the woman on the left), and between 1868 and 1874 Manet painted a series of eleven portraits of her.

The Balcony was chosen for the 1869 Salon. When Berthe arrived at the exhibition, Manet was emotionally overwrought, worried about the reception his work would receive. "There I found Manet, with his hat on in bright sunlight, looking dazed," she said. "He begged me to go and see his painting, as he did not dare to move a step. I have never seen such an expressive face as his; he was laughing, then had a worried look, assuring everybody that his picture was very bad, and adding in the same breath that it would be a great success. I think he has a decidedly charming temperament, I like it very much."[4]

Typically, most critics did not like *The Balcony*. By this time, Manet accepted the negative reactions with weary resignation and found solace by continuing to work.

During the Franco-Prussian War, which lasted from July 1870 to May 1871, Manet sent his family to the French countryside to keep them away from the fighting in and around Paris. He joined the National Guard and served as a gunner. Although he generally did not have any interest in historical paintings, the horror of war affected him deeply, as reflected in the paintings *Execution of Maximilian, Civil War* and *The Barricade*. In early February 1871, Manet joined his family in Oloron-Sainte-Marie, located in southwest France near the Pyrenees. Later that month he went to Bordeaux, where he painted *The Port of Bordeaux*.

Portrait of Berthe Morisot, 1872. After she married Eugéne, Manet and Berthe burned each other's love letters.

Manet painted *The Port of Bordeaux* in 1871.

When the war ended in May, Manet and Suzanne returned to Paris, but he didn't stay long. Stressed by the war and his ongoing struggles with being accepted by the mainstream Parisian art community, Édouard took a solo vacation to Bologne, a port city on the English Channel. When he finally settled back into Parisian life, Manet and his artist friends again gathered for their regular get-togethers. They eventually abandoned the Café Guerbois and adopted another Montmartre hangout, Nouvelle Athénes.

There was another change that deeply affected Manet's life. In 1874 Berthe married brother Eugéne Manet, who was deeply supportive of her painting career. Afterward, Berthe and Édouard burned each other's letters, indicating whatever physical and personal intimate relationship they had was officially over. Perhaps most telling was that, although they remained close friends, after she married his brother, Édouard never painted another picture of Berthe.

Edgar Degas

Edgar Degas,
Self-Portrait

Although Edgar Degas is honored as a founder of Impressionism, he personally considered himself a realist, like Manet.

Hilaire Germain Edgar Degas was born in Paris on July 19, 1834. His father, Auguste, was a wealthy French banker; his mother, Célestine, was from New Orleans. His parents sent him to the Lycée Louis-le-Grand when he was eleven. Edgar graduated in 1853 with a degree in literature.

By then he had already developed a deep interest in art, particularly historical themes, and turned a room of the family house into his painting studio. But just like Manet's father, Auguste Degas expected his son to be a lawyer, so Edgar enrolled in law school. And just like Manet, Edgar was a disinterested student. In April 1855, Degas was admitted to L'École des Beaux-Arts. The following year he left for Italy and stayed for three years copying the works of Michelangelo and other Renaissance artists. He returned to Paris in 1859 and had his first Salon showing in 1865 with *Scene of War in the Middle Ages*. His paintings were selected for the next five years, and over that time his interest in history was replaced by more contemporary subjects—a direct influence of Manet, whom he met in 1862 while copying paintings at the Louvre. They quickly became friends and friendly rivals. They shared a similar background and education but differed in their ambition. Manet wanted to be famous and wanted the respect of critics—a trait for which Degas frequently needled Manet because it was one of the primary reasons for Manet's ongoing angst.

Degas was most prolific between 1873 and 1883. Hallmarks of his work were his experimentation with perspective and angles, and ballerinas with featureless faces. Some art historians suspect Degas adapted his style to accommodate his failing eyesight. While in the National Guard he had been diagnosed with degenerative eye disease, possibly macular degeneration.

After 1874, Degas stopped exhibiting at the Salon, choosing to show his work with the Impressionists instead. As his eyesight failed, he became a recluse. He died blind and alone in Paris on September 27, 1917.

Degas' *The Dancers*

Gare Saint-Lazare (The Railway) was the last time Manet painted Victorine Meurent. When the painting was exhibited at the 1874 Salon, critics found the unconventional depth of field confusing.

An Untimely End

There are several elements that made Impressionism not just unique but revolutionary. First and foremost was the use of light and color. For example, instead of mixing blue and yellow paint to make green, they put yellow paint next to blue paint. When viewers looked at the canvas, their brain would still "see" green, or the *impression* of green. The overall sense, or essence, of the painting was more important than the details of it. Also, the use of black paint was avoided. Short brushstrokes were used instead of the bold strokes of classical painting. And up until the Impressionists, painting was done indoors—even landscapes were done inside a studio. The Impressionists worked *en plein air,* meaning they worked outside, which allowed them to better capture the effects of sunlight. It was a central Impressionist belief that one could find true art only by painting directly from nature.

Manet often found inspiration from simply walking down the street and seeing the daily life of Parisians, whether they were upper-class ladies or the homeless. In 1873, he painted *The Gare Saint-Lazare. (The Railway).* The painting is notable for both its unconventional depth of field and because it was the last time he painted Victorine Meurent. A brochure that accompanied a Manet showing at a 1998 exhibition says that when the painting was exhibited at the 1874 Salon, "Visitors and critics found its subject baffling, its composition incoherent, and its execution sketchy. Caricaturists ridiculed Manet's picture, in which only a few recognized the symbol of modernity that it has become today."[1]

It's easy to see why the Impressionists considered Manet a kind of spiritual mentor. He was a serious artist who rejected the traditional restrictions and constraints of the art mainstream in order to follow his own unique vision. His willingness to experiment and try new techniques at the cost of reputation and commercial success was an inspiration to the group. Ironically, though, for as much as Manet craved appreciation for his work, he did not enthusiastically embrace his role of revolutionary, mostly because he did not consider himself particularly avant-garde. And while many of the Impressionists didn't care about being accepted by the mainstream, Manet did, which is why he did not participate when the Impressionists held their first exhibition in 1874 or in any of those that followed. Instead, he remained committed to the Salon. Even when the Salon jury rejected *The Artist* and *The Laundress* in 1875, Manet exhibited them along with other paintings in his studio rather than exhibit with the Impressionists.

Despite his reluctance to have his art classified, Manet still actively supported the Impressionists. On a personal level, he even gave some of

Monet self-portrait, 1886

them financial assistance. Nor was he adverse to experimenting with en plein air. In the summer of 1875, Manet wrote Théodore Duret: "I went to see Monet yesterday and found him in despair and absolutely broke. He asked me to find someone who would take between ten and twenty pictures of their choice for 100 francs a piece. Shall we do the deal ourselves, putting up 500 francs each? Of course no one, and least of all he, should know that we're in on this."[2]

Although they had known each other since 1866, Manet had become

close to Monet only a year earlier. Manet began accompanying Monet on outdoor painting excursions. It was during this time that Manet incorporated more elements of Impressionism, something Berthe Morisot had been urging him to do for years. Up to then, Manet had only worked in his studio, but Berthe thought he should go outdoors and try his hand with brighter colors. The result was a series of paintings that some art historians considered Manet's Middle Period, including *Monet Working on His Boat*, *Boating*, *The Grand Canal in Venice* and *Argenteuil.* But his experimentation with Impressionism essentially ended with Berthe's marriage to his brother, and Édouard never fully adopted the style.

Manet's *Monet Working on His Boat* was painted en plein air.

In addition to his canvases, Monet also occasionally illustrated books. In 1875 he created five etchings for the French language edition of Edgar Allan Poe's *The Raven*, called *Le Corbeau*. Only 240 copies of the edition were published, but it was a critical success. The reviewer for the Paris Journal wrote:

> The artist has translated, by a remarkably vigorous handling of the black and white medium, the multiple, fantastic shapes of the sinister bird. Through the apparent but carefully calculated roughness and lack of finish in the technique, through the interplay of abrupt silhouettes and threatening shadows, M. Manet has transposed from one art into another the nightmare atmosphere and hallucinations that are so powerfully expressed in the works of Edgar Poe.[3]

Despite the rave reviews, the edition was a commercial failure.

In the late 1870s, Manet went back to painting indoor scenes, although he continued to incorporate elements of Impressionism in his work, such as in *Brasserie de Reichshoffen*. The result was a blending of style that is uniquely Manet. Many art experts believe Manet achieved the perfect blend of those two styles in his 1882 masterpiece *A Bar at the Folies-Bergère*. As in *Olympia*, the woman in the picture appears to be aloof—even though the reflection in the mirror reveals she is talking to a customer, her expression is enigmatic. It's as if Manet is showing two different sides of her personality.

In 1881 the French government awarded Manet the prestigious Legion of Honor, but by this time his health was failing. At first, Manet thought he had developed arthritis, but in reality he was suffering from syphilis. Although he had contracted the disease as a young man, it had finally advanced into its final stage. Walking became increasingly difficult, as did holding paint brushes. Toward the end of his life he began painting with watercolors because the small brush was easier to hold. He was in constant pain and, like his father, suffered from partial paralysis. By April 1883

His 1882 masterpiece *A Bar at the Folies-Bergère* blends Manet's eye for realism with elements of Impressionism.

he was bedridden, unable to walk at all. Doctors amputated his left leg, which had turned gangrenous, in an attempt to save his life, but he died eleven days later, on April 30. He was only fifty-one years old.

Although his career spanned a mere two decades, Manet is credited with being one of the greatest innovators in art. The simplicity of his style, his bold use of light, and his use of contemporary subjects inspired generations of artists to break away from artistic traditions. Manet was a visionary who incorporated elements of both Realism and Impressionism and in so doing laid the foundation for new styles to come. He cemented his place in history as the father of Modernism.

Monet

Oscar-Claude Monet was born in Paris on November 14, 1840, but grew up in Le Havre, on the Normandy coast. His father was a grocer who also sold supplies for sailboats. In the late 1850s, Monet met Eugéne Boudin, a landscape artist who introduced him to the idea of painting outside in natural light. Monet would later say he owed his career to Boudin.

In 1860, Monet attended the Académie Suisse in Paris, then enrolled two years later in the studio of Charles Gleyre. His classmates included Pierre-Auguste Renoir, Frédéric Bazille, and other future Impressionists. He had his first Salon showing in 1865, but was not successful enough to earn a living from art. Unable to support himself, Monet was forced to leave Paris and his pregnant girlfriend, Camille-Léonie Doncieux, and move back to Le Havre in 1867. When he was able to return, he married Camille in 1870. Despite their financial difficulties, she remained supportive of his art.

Although the Salon had shown some of his work, it also rejected many of his paintings. Monet joined Renoir, Edgar Degas, Camille Pissarro, and others in establishing an independent exhibition in 1874. His painting *Impression: Sunrise* was particularly attacked by critics. Reviewer Louis Leroy ridiculed the unorthodox style: "Impression—I was certain of it. I was just telling myself that, since I was impressed, there had to be some impression in it . . . and what freedom, what ease of workmanship! Wallpaper in its embryonic state is more finished than that seascape."[4] After that, Monet and the others became known as the Impressionists.

Monet continued to struggle financially through the 1870s. Camille died of tuberculosis in 1879, and later Monet married Alice Hoschedé. It wasn't until the late 1880s that Monet's work received critical acclaim. In 1890 he could finally afford to buy a home in Giverny, 40 miles outside of Paris.

Monet was extremely prolific and continued painting until very shortly before his death on December 5, 1926. Because he left behind so many paintings, examples of his work hang in nearly every major art museum and gallery in the world.

Monet's *Water Lilies*, 1916

CHAPTER NOTES

Chapter 1. Très Scandal

1. PBS.org. *The Shock of the Nude: Manet's Olympia* http://www.pbs.org/wgbh/cultureshock/beyond/manet.html
2. Jeffrey Meyer, *Impressionist Quartet: The Intimate Genius of Manet and Morisot, Degas and Cassatt* (New York: Harcourt, 2005), p. 37.
3. Salon.com, *Manet's Olympia* http://dir.salon.com/story/ent/masterpiece/2002/05/13/olympia
4. Monica Bohm-Duchen, *The Private Life of a Masterpiece* (Berkeley, CA: University of California Press, 2002), p. 118.
5. PBS.org. *The Shock of the Nude: Manet's Olympia* http://www.pbs.org/wgbh/cultureshock/beyond/manet.html
6. Paul Hayes Tucker, *Manet's Le Déjeuner sur l'Herbe* (New York: Cambridge University Press, 1998), p. 12.

Chapter 2. Unlikely Provocateur

1. Jeffrey Meyers, *Impressionist Quartet: The Intimate Genius of Manet and Morisot, Degas and Cassatt* (New York: Harcourt, 2005), p. 3.
2. Beth Archer Brombert, *Edouard Manet* (Chicago: University of Chicago Press, 1996), p. 18.
3. Meyers, p. 6.
4. Brombert, p. 28.
5. Ibid., p. 27.
6. Edwin Stowe, *Velazquez*, Verlag von G. U. Ceemann., 1881, Original from Oxford University, Digitized June 19, 2006.

Chapter 3. Early Works

1. Jeffrey Meyer, *Impressionist Quartet: The Intimate Genius of Manet and Morisot, Degas and Cassatt* (New York: Harcourt, 2005), p. 8.

2. Georges Bataille, *Manet* (New York: Albert Skira, 1955), p. 7.
3. Meyer, p. 10.
4. Ibid., p. 15.
5. Svetlana Alpers, *The Vexation of Art* (New Haven, CT: Yale University Press, 2005), p. 221.
6. Ibid., p. 226.
7. Meyer, p. 23.
8. G. H. Hamilton. *Manet and His Critics*, New Haven, Connecticut: Yale University Press, 1986, pg 93 (article originally published in *Revue du XIX e siècle* of January 1, 1867).

Chapter 4. Inspirations

1. Georges Bataille, *Manet* (New York: Albert Skira, 1955), p. 10.
2. Jeffrey Meyer, *Impressionist Quartet: The Intimate Genius of Manet and Morisot, Degas and Cassatt* (New York: Harcourt, 2005), p. 54.
3. Bataille, p. 24.
4. Jeffrey Meyer, "Morisot & Manet," *New Criterion*, January 1, 2005, http://www.highbeam.com/doc/1G1-127542486.html

Chapter 5. An Untimely End

1. Isabelle Dervaux, *Manet, Monet, and the Gare Saint-Lazare* (Washington, DC: National Gallery of Art, 1998), p. 1.
2. Manet's Letters—Letter to Duret, http://www.mystudios.com/manet/letters/letter-duret-1875.html
3. Kevin J. Hayes, *The Cambridge Companion to Edgar Allan Poe* (New York: Cambridge University Press, 2002), p. 227.
4. Louis Leroy, "L'exposition des impressionnistes," *Charivari*, April 25, 1874, pp. 2–3.

CHRONOLOGY

1832   Édouard Manet is born in Paris on January 23
1844   He attends Rollin College, where he befriends Antonin Proust
1848   Manet embarks on voyage to Rio de Janeiro
1850   He studies with Thomas Couture
1855   Manet meets Delacroix
1856   He sets up his own art studio
1858   Manet meets Charles Baudelaire
1859   *The Absinthe Drinker* is turned down by the Salon
1860   Manet moves in with Suzanne Leenhoff and her son Léon
1861   *M. and Mme. Auguste Manet* and *The Spanish Singer* are shown at the Salon
1862   Auguste Manet, Édouard's father, dies
1863   Édouard marries Suzanne Leenhoff; *Le Déjeuner sur l'Herbe* is shown at Salon des Refusés
1865   After the *Olympia* scandal, Manet travels to Spain
1868   He meets Berthe Morisot
1870   Manet joins the National Guard during the Franco-Prussian War; he duels with Duranty
1874   Manet spends the summer painting with Monet in Argenteuil
1881   Manet receives Legion of Honor award
1882   *A Bar at the Folies-Bergère* is shown at the Salon
1883   Manet dies on April 30 of complications from syphilis
1884   École des Beaux-Arts holds a Manet exhibit in January
1893   *Olympia* becomes part of the Louvre art museum's permanent collection

SELECTED PAINTINGS

1858	*The Boy with Cherries*	1873	*On the Beach*
1860	*M. and Mme. Auguste Manet*	1874	*Argenteuil*
1861	*Boy with Dog*		*Boating*
1863	*Olympia*		*Claude Monet Working on His Boat in Argenteuil*
1867	*The Execution of the Emperor Maximilian*	1879	*Chez le Père Lathuile*
1868	*Portrait of Émile Zola*	1880	*A Bunch of Asparagus*
1868–69	*The Balcony*		*Portrait of Antonin Proust*
1872	*Portrait of Berthe Morisot*	1882	*A Bar at the Folies-Bergère*
1873	*Gare Saint-Lazare (The Railway)*		*Autumn*

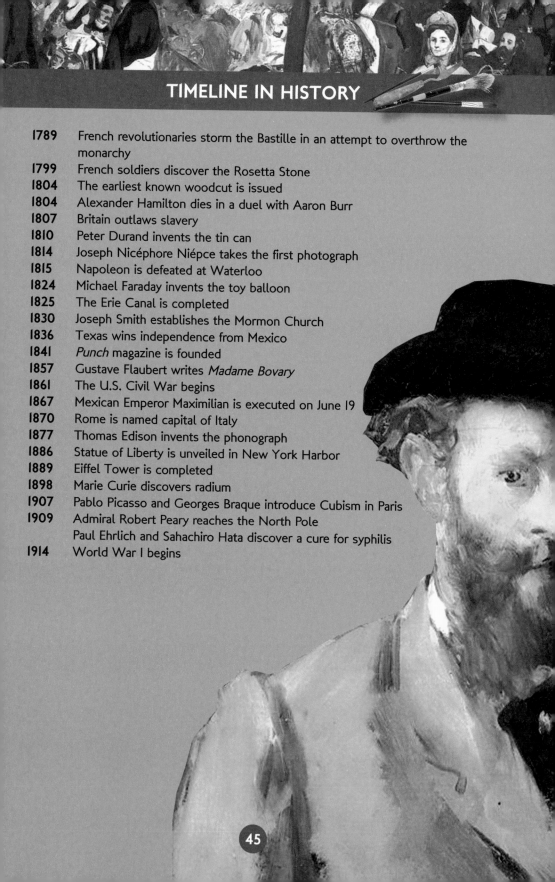

TIMELINE IN HISTORY

1789	French revolutionaries storm the Bastille in an attempt to overthrow the monarchy
1799	French soldiers discover the Rosetta Stone
1804	The earliest known woodcut is issued
1804	Alexander Hamilton dies in a duel with Aaron Burr
1807	Britain outlaws slavery
1810	Peter Durand invents the tin can
1814	Joseph Nicéphore Niépce takes the first photograph
1815	Napoleon is defeated at Waterloo
1824	Michael Faraday invents the toy balloon
1825	The Erie Canal is completed
1830	Joseph Smith establishes the Mormon Church
1836	Texas wins independence from Mexico
1841	*Punch* magazine is founded
1857	Gustave Flaubert writes *Madame Bovary*
1861	The U.S. Civil War begins
1867	Mexican Emperor Maximilian is executed on June 19
1870	Rome is named capital of Italy
1877	Thomas Edison invents the phonograph
1886	Statue of Liberty is unveiled in New York Harbor
1889	Eiffel Tower is completed
1898	Marie Curie discovers radium
1907	Pablo Picasso and Georges Braque introduce Cubism in Paris
1909	Admiral Robert Peary reaches the North Pole
	Paul Ehrlich and Sahachiro Hata discover a cure for syphilis
1914	World War I begins

FURTHER READING

Books

Mis, Melody S. *Édouard Manet.* New York: PowerKids Press, 2007.

Spence, David. *Manet.* Kent, England: Ticktock Media, Ltd., 2004.

Whiting, Jim. *Claude Monet.* Hockessin, DE: Mitchell Lane Publishers, 2007.

Wright, Patricia. *Eyewitness: Manet.* New York: DK Publishing, 2000.

Works Consulted

Alpers, Svetlana. *The Vexations of Art: Velazquez and Others.* New Haven, CT: Yale University Press, 2005.

Bataille, Georges. *Manet.* New York: Albert Skira, 1955.

Bohm-Duchen, Monica. *The Private Life of a Masterpiece: Uncovering the Forgotten Secrets and Hidden Life Histories of Iconic Works of Art.* Berkeley, CA: University of California Press, 2002.

British Museum, Antonin Proust
http://www.britishmuseum.org/explore/highlights/highlight_objects/ pd/a/anders_zorn,_antonin_proust,_a.aspx

Brombert, Beth Archer. *Edouard Manet: Rebel in a Frock Coat.* Chicago: University of Chicago Press, 1996.

Hamilton, G. H. *Manet and His Critics.* New Haven, CT: Yale University Press, 1986.

Hayes, Kevin J. *The Cambridge Companion to Edgar Allan Poe.* Cambridge, MA: Cambridge University Press, 2002.

Manet's Letters, Letter to Duret.
http://www.mystudios.com/manet/letters/letter-duret-1875.html

Meyer, Jeffrey. *Impressionist Quartet: The Intimate Genius of Manet and Morisot, Degas and Cassatt.* New York: Harcourt, 2005.

Meyer, Jeffrey. "Morisot & Manet," *New Criterion*, January 1, 2005.
http://www.highbeam.com/doc/1G1-127542486.html

PBS.org, *The Shock of the Nude: Manet's Olympia.*
http://www.pbs.org/wgbh/cultureshock/beyond/manet.html

Salon.com, *Manet's Olympia.*
http://dir.salon.com/story/ent/masterpiece/2002/05/13/olympia

Stowe, Edwin. *Velazquez.* Verlag von G. U. Ceemann, 1881. Original from Oxford University, Digitized June 19, 2006.

Tucker, Paul Hayes. *Manet's Le Déjeuner sur l'Herbe.* New York: Cambridge University Press, 1998.

FURTHER READING

On the Internet

Artchive.com, Édouard Manet
   http://www.artchive.com/artchive/M/manet.html
National Gallery of Art, Édouard Manet and his Influence
   http://www.nga.gov/collection/gallery/gg90/gg90-main1.html
Web Museum, Édouard Manet
   http://www.ibiblio.org/wm/paint/auth/manet/

GLOSSARY

aphasia (uh-FAY-zhuh)—Loss of the ability to speak.

avant-garde (AH-vahnt-gard)—A style or school in the arts that is considered to be a radical departure from what is traditional.

baroque (bah-ROHK)—A painting style that emphasizes irregular, complex forms.

bohemian (boh-HEE-mee-un)—Unconventional, or someone who lives an unconventional life; most often refers to artists or other creative people.

caricature (KAH-rih-kuh-chur)—A picture of a person that exaggerates the person's features.

cause célèbre (kawz seh-LEB)—Something notorious; an issue that creates widespread interest and strong opinions.

debacle (deh-BAH-kul)—A total failure.

debauchery (dih-BAW-chuh-ree)—Immoral behavior.

dowry (DOW-ree)—The cash and assets a husband receives from his bride's family on their marriage.

gangrenous (GANG-greh-nus)—Showing signs of gangrene, a condition in which parts of the skin die.

homage (AH-mij)—An expression of high regard or respect.

illegitimate (il-uh-JIH-tih-mit)—Born to a mother who is not married to the father.

introspective (in-troh-SPEK-tiv)—Thoughtful self-examination.

juxtaposition (juk-stuh-poh-ZIH-shun)—The placement of two or more objects next to or near each other.

macular degeneration (MAA-kyuh-lur dee-jeh-ner-AY-shun)—The gradual breakdown of the tissue at the back of the eye, causing loss of vision.

mannerism (MAA-nur-ism)—A painting style characterized by distortions of scale and perspective.

old master—A painter of note who lived prior to the nineteenth century.

parochial (puh-ROH-kee-ul) **school**—A private school run by a church.

provocateur (proh-VAH-kuh-TOOR)—A person who causes trouble; an agitator.

INDEX

Absinthe Drinker, The 22, 23, 31

Artist, The 38

Balcony, The 32, 33

Bar at the Folies-Bergère, A 40–41

Barricade, The 33

Baudelaire, Charles-Pierre 10, 22, 24, 25, 27

Bazille, Frédéric 29–30, 42

Boy with Cherries, The 22

Café Guerbois 29, 30, 31, 34

Cézanne, Paul 29

Civil War 33

Collardet 31

Couture, Thomas 11, 21, 22, 23

Degas, Edgar 10, 29, 30, 35, 42

Déjeuner sur l'Herbe, Le (The Picnic) 6, 7, 9, 10, 11, 24

Duranty, Louis 29–31

Duret, Théodore 24, 25, 26, 29, 38

Execution of Maximilian 33

Fantin-Latour, Henri 31

Fleurs du Mal, Les 27

Fournier, Edmond 14, 15, 18

Franco-Prussian War 33

Gare Saint-Lazare (The Railway) 10, 36, 37

Havre et Guadeloupe 16

Impressionism 28, 29, 31, 35, 37–38, 39, 40, 42

Laundress, The 38

Leenhoff, Suzanne 25, 34

Louvre Museum 15, 22

M. and Mme. Auguste Manet 12, 24

Manet, Auguste (father) 12, 13–14, 15, 18, 22, 23, 24, 25

Manet, Éduoard
and assistant's suicide 22

birth of 13

in Brazil 16–18

childhood of 13–14

death of 41

and duel 30–31

education of 14–15, 21–22

marriage of 25

and Middle Period 39

in National Guard 33, 34

naval career of 15–18

siblings of 13

and syphilis 40

Manet, Eugène (brother) 11, 13, 34

Manet, Eugénie Désirée (mother) 12, 13, 15, 16

Meninas, Las 25

Meurent, Victorine 10, 11, 36, 37

Modernism 41

Monet, Claude 11, 29, 38–40, 42

Monet Working on His Boat 39

Morisot, Berthe 31, 32, 33–34, 39

Nouvelle Athénes 34

Olympia 8–9, 10, 11, 24, 25, 40

Philosopher, The 28, 30

Pissarro, Camille 29–30, 42

Poe, Edgar Allan 40

Port of Bordeaux, The 33, 34

Proust, Antonin 9, 11, 14, 21, 29

Renoir, Pierre-Auguste 29, 42

The Romans of the Decadence 21, 23

Salon 6, 7, 21, 24, 26, 33, 35, 36, 37

Salon des Refusés 7–8, 11

Spanish Singer, The 24

Street Singer, The 10

Velázquez, Diego 15, 19, 22, 25–26, 28

Zola, Émile 24, 26, 29, 31